110637637

GENEVA PRESS EDITORIAL BOARD

Louis B. Weeks, president, Union Theological Seminary in Virginia
Robert Benedetto, Union Theological Seminary in Virginia
John M. Buchanan, pastor, Fourth Presbyterian Church, Chicago
W. Stacy Johnson, Austin Presbyterian Theological Seminary
Douglas F. Ottati, Union Theological Seminary in Virginia
Ann B. Weems, Presbyterian poet and educator, St. Louis
Beverly Zink-Sawyer, Union Theological Seminary in Virginia

Geneva Press, an imprint of the Presbyterian Publishing Corporation in collaboration with Union Theological Seminary in Virginia, is devoted to providing resources in the Reformed tradition dealing with the history, theology, and life of the Presbyterian Church (U.S.A.).

Sealed in Christ

Sealed in Christ

The Symbolism of the Seal of the
PRESBYTERIAN CHURCH (U.S.A.)

John M. Mulder

Geneva Press
Louisville, Kentucky

© 1991 John M. Mulder
Presbyterian Church (U.S.A.)

All rights reserved

No part of this book may be reproduced in any form without
permission in writing from the publisher, except by a reviewer who
wishes to quote brief passages in connection with a review in a
magazine or newspaper.

Scripture quotations are from the New Revised Standard Version of
the Bible and are copyrighted © 1989 by the Division of Christian
Education of the National Council of the Churches of Christ in the
U.S.A. and are used by permission.

Book Design: Malcolm Grear Designers

First edition

Printed in the United States of America

9 8 7 6 5 4 3

ISBN 0-664-50004-8

For Aaron and Cora

"It is God who establishes us with you in Christ

and has anointed us;

by putting his seal on us

and giving us his Spirit in our hearts as a first installment."

2 Corinthians 1:21

Contents

PREFACE

This short book is the product of one of the most enjoyable experiences of my life as a Presbyterian. In 1983, I was asked to chair a task force that presented the seal of the newly reunited Presbyterian Church (U.S.A.) to the General Assembly for approval. The Assembly unanimously ratified the design in 1985.

The experience proved to be exciting and stimulating, for the task force included a remarkably talented group of theologians, pastors, educators, musicians, and artists. The group included Nancy Chinn, an artist in San Anselmo, Calif.; the Rev. Calvin W. Didier, pastor of House of Hope Presbyterian Church, St. Paul, Minn.; Dr. Theodore A. Gill, theologian and ethicist at John Jay College, City University of New York; Lucille Hair, organist and choir director at University Presbyterian Church, Baton Rouge, La.; Wynn McGregor, a worship leader and Christian educator from Corpus Christi, Texas; the Rev. Neil Severance, vice-president and dean of students at the Rhode Island School of Design; and Dr. Leo F. Twiggs, professor of art at South Carolina State College, Orangeburg, S.C. The Rev. Mary B. McNamara, staff associate of the General Assembly Council of the Presbyterian Church (U.S.A.), assisted the task force and brought to her work both administrative efficiency and theological and artistic insight.

The mandate for the task force was ambiguous. At the 1983 General Assembly, a symbol by Texas designer James Avery had been presented as an interim seal of the church. Mr. Avery had produced an attractive design in the incredibly short three or four months between the approval of reunion by the presbyteries and the meeting of the General Assembly. A commissioner moved that the Avery design become the new seal of the reunited church. Another commissioner moved a typical Presbyterian alternative: appoint a committee to study the proposed seal and make a recommendation. Thus began the life of the task force on the seal.

At first I hoped the task force would move quickly to ratify the Avery design, but in the first two hours of our first meeting, it became obvious from the responses we received from Presbyterians across the nation and from the verdict of the task force members that an easy solution was not to be. We then began to work along two lines: first, we had to decide what we wanted represented in the seal—both its symbols and its qualities; second, we had to select a designer.

We initiated a national search for a designer and finally selected Malcolm Grear, one of America's preeminent graphic designers. He serves as professor of graphic design at the Rhode Island School of Design as well as president of his own company, Malcolm Grear Designers. His clients have included the Guggenheim Museum, the Metropolitan Opera in New York, the U.S. Department of Health and Human Services, the Department of Veterans Affairs, as well as many corporations and nonprofit institutions. His consultant on the project was Dr. Martha Gregor Goethals, a distinguished designer and art historian who also teaches at the Rhode Island School of Design. Trained in theology and art at Yale, the Massachusetts Institute of Technology, and Harvard, she assisted Grear and his associates, as well as the task force, in exploring the depth and range of Christian symbols that could be used in the new seal.

The task force argued intensely about what the seal should include. Several members pointed to the antipathy to symbolism in the Presbyterian tradition, and indeed they were right. Until the 1890s none of the Presbyterian churches in the United States had a symbol or seal. This iconoclasm was rooted in the Reformed emphasis on the priority of the Word, the attempt to rid the church of any Roman Catholic imagery, and the fear of idolatry. But gradually we recognized the iconoclastic impulse in the Reformed tradition as a resource. Simplicity rules as the dominant philosophy of design and symbolism today. Less is more, or more is communicated by stating less. A willingness to accept the iconoclasm of the past opened the task force to designs that would be simultaneously classic and contemporary.

We saw also that the seal should be a mini-confession—a symbolic and graphic statement of central theological affirmations of the Presbyterian Church (U.S.A.). Since another committee was working on developing a statement of faith for the reunited church, we were compelled to forge our own theological position—at least for the purpose of telling Malcolm Grear and Martha Gregor Goethals what we wanted included in the symbolism of the seal.

Some of us highlighted the pluralism of the church and wondered whether any set of symbols could capture that diversity. Some of us considered the Presbyterian form of government as the distinctive characteristic of Presbyterianism, and wondered how that could be captured. Finally, we decided on certain basic symbols and images that had to be included.

The cross was immediately identified as the single most important image because of its centrality throughout the history of the church and its currency as the most ecumenical of Christian symbols. The task force also thought that the Trinity should be represented as well as the relationship between the Holy Spirit and the Word. Because of the frequency in which flames or fire appeared in earlier Presbyterian seals and because of the multifaceted meaning of fire in the Christian tradition, we stipulated that fire should be an essential element in the new design. The task force also hoped to find some way of symbolizing the representative form of Presbyterian government and the importance of covenant as a theological idea.

We feared we would get a "busy" design, which we did not want. We wanted a seal that would have continuity with the historic symbols of the Reformed tradition and the larger

Christian tradition but also would be contemporary. We believed it should have a timeless quality and avoid temporary theological themes. It should be easily understood and graphically flexible, attractive in color as well as in black and white, discernible as a very small image or on a large scale. The task force rejected the use of mottos, believing that the design should not be dependent on words for its statement and its meaning. We stressed that the design should have an emotive, evocative character, suggesting the vitality of the mission of the church; and yet it should be more formal than informal in nature and have a "structural" or "ordered" quality. Finally, the task force stated that the new seal should not be divisive for the church.

We submitted that content and those qualities, enveloped in often self-contradictory hopes, to Mr. Grear and his associates. What we received was everything we asked for and more. The design proved to be a simple but eloquent statement of the Presbyterian Church's heritage, identity, and mission. We requested four possible designs. When Mr. Grear first presented them, this task force composed of diverse minds, immediately and with near unanimity picked the present design.

After more than four thousand drawings of the seal and its various parts, Mr. Grear and his associates presented the final version to the General Assembly in Indianapolis in 1985. He confessed to me in advance how worried he was to have seven hundred Presbyterians *voting* on his art! Bill Gee of the General Assembly staff had prepared a powerful video presentation of the seal, accompanied by two hymns—"How Firm a Foundation" and "Amazing Grace." After the video was played and the lights came up, the Assembly rose to give Mr. Grear and Dr. Goethals a standing ovation. Mr. Grear burst into tears.

For those of us who were fortunate enough to be a part of the creation of the seal, it was an experience of grace. The seal has now been widely accepted across the church and used in a staggering variety of ways and on many different objects—from church bulletins and signs to needlework, ties, and jackets.

Since then I have used the seal to teach people the meaning of the Presbyterian tradition, and I have been intrigued by the way the seal itself engages people's imaginations and helps them to understand the content and imagery of the Bible and the abstractions of doctrine and theology. Slowly it dawned on me that perhaps a short exposition of the seal's symbolism might be useful to the church for communicants' classes, the training of new members and officers, and in other ways. What follows is my effort to draw out some of the biblical and theological themes symbolized in the seal.

It should be noted that all the symbols associated with the Presbyterian seal can be found in other religions, in antiquity, and even in secular culture. Neither Christianity in its various forms or the Reformed and Presbyterian tradition has a monopoly on the symbols of the cross, the dove, fire, water, and so on. This in no way diminishes the meaning of the symbols we associate with this multiform seal. In fact, it can be said that just because the Presbyterian symbols tie in with other expressions of the same symbols, we can rejoice that our faith, while special and historic in its own right, makes common cause with God's universal symbolic language.

5

I want to thank Malcolm Grear, Martha Gregor Goethals, and each member of the task force for the opportunity to work with them. I also want to thank the library staffs of Louisville Presbyterian Theological Seminary and Western Theological Seminary for their help in preparing this volume. Several colleagues read drafts of the book and provided helpful comments and criticism. They include Milton J. Coalter, Burton Cooper, Virgil Cruz, Hugh T. Kerr, W. Eugene March, Clinton D. Morrison, Marion S. Soards, and Louis B. Weeks. I particularly want to thank Keith Cardwell, who helped me with some of

the research, and Andy Meeker, Kem Longino, Jean New-
man, and Dana Cormack.

My wife, Mary, and I have two children, Aaron and Cora,
and this book is dedicated to them. Like other children they
found the seal intriguing, and in the weeks before its presentation to the General Assembly, they were fond of sketching
it for me and talking about its meaning. When I told Cora
about writing this book, she declared, "That's neat!" I hope it
will be so for others.

John M. Mulder

THE CROSS

The center of the seal of the Presbyterian Church (U.S.A.) consists of the cross—the universal symbol of the Christian faith. The cross captures the heart of the Christian gospel, the message that in the death and resurrection of Jesus Christ we see God's love and we are offered forgiveness from our sins: "For God so loved the world that he gave his only Son, so that everyone who believes in him may not perish but may have eternal life" (John 3:16). At first, the early Christians did not use the cross as a sign of devotion to Christ, probably because it was a "stumbling block to Jews and foolishness to Gentiles" (1 Cor. 1:23) or because it so clearly identified someone as a follower of Christ and thereby brought persecution.

The conversion of the emperor Constantine in A.D. 312 included a vision of a flaming cross in the sky with the words "by this sign conquer," and Constantine encouraged the public display of the cross as the symbol of Christianity. From the fourth century to the present, the cross has been widely used in Christianity to depict the essential affirmations of the Christian faith.

As a physical object, the cross refers to the death of Jesus on a tree with a cross bar. All four Gospels tell the story (Matt. 27; Mark 15; Luke 23; John 19), and Christ's death on a cross or a tree is mentioned many times throughout the New Testament. The method of his execution—crucifixion—was widely used in the Roman empire for criminals. It placed Jesus under the ancient curse mentioned by Paul in Galatians. Paul quoted the Old Testament: "for it is written, 'Cursed is everyone who hangs on a tree'" (Gal. 3:13; cf. Deut. 21:23).

Here stands the central assertion of Christianity: God was fully human in Jesus Christ to the point of suffering and dying

9

an ignoble death on the cross. But God raised Jesus Christ from the dead to bring forgiveness and new life to humanity with God through the risen Christ. One of the oldest hymns or creeds of the Christian church summarizes this fundamental Christian belief in Philippians 2:

> Let the same mind be in you that was in Christ Jesus, who, though he was in the form of God, did not regard equality with God as something to be exploited, but emptied himself, taking the form of a slave, being born in human likeness. And being found in human form, he humbled himself and became obedient to the point of death, even death on a cross. Therefore God also highly exalted him and gave him the name that is above every name, so that at the name of Jesus every knee should bend, in heaven and on earth and under the earth, and every tongue should confess that Jesus Christ is Lord, to the glory of God the Father (2:5–11).

The cross as a symbol of Christianity embodies both the suffering of Christ and the triumph of God over sin and death. Through the cross, we are made at one with God. This paradox of life amidst death, and power through weakness, remains a primary theme in Paul's letters and the proclamation of the early Christians. In Corinthians, Paul declared that he "decided to know nothing among you except Jesus Christ, and him crucified" (1 Cor. 2:2). Paul also proclaimed that the cross is the center of his preaching: "For Christ did not send me to baptize but to proclaim the gospel, and not with eloquent wisdom, so that the cross of Christ might not be emptied of its power. For the message about the cross is foolishness to those who are perishing, but to us who are being saved it is the power of God" (1 Cor. 1:17–18).

Throughout the preaching and teaching of the church, the cross has symbolized God's love in Jesus Christ. We may know God in many different ways, but at the heart of the Christian gospel is the affirmation in First John: "God is love" (4:8).

Indeed, the Gospel and letters of John repeatedly emphasize the centrality of God's love. It is God's love that binds us to God and to one another: "Beloved, let us love one another, because love is from God; everyone who loves is born of God and knows God. Whoever does not love does not know God, for God is love. God's love was revealed among us in this way: God sent his only Son into the world so that we might live through him. In this is love, not that we loved God but that he loved us and sent his Son to be the atoning sacrifice for our sins. Beloved, since God loved us so much, we also ought to love one another. No one has ever seen God; if we love one another, God lives in us, and his love is perfected in us" (1 John 4:7–12).

In Jesus Christ, we know God's final and complete word to the brokenness and sin of the world—love, the sacrificial love of God in Jesus Christ on the cross—and through that love we are reconciled and reunited with God and with others. The beautiful hymn of Isaac Watts, "When I Survey the Wondrous Cross," captures this affirmation:

> Were the whole realm of nature mine,
> That were a present far too small;
> Love so amazing, so divine,
> Demands my soul, my life, my all.

The Christian gospel proclaims the forgiving and abiding love of God in Jesus Christ, and a widely told story of the great theologian Karl Barth illustrates this central truth. Toward the end of his career and after many learned theological treatises, Barth was reportedly asked to summarize his entire theology in one sentence. He paused and then quoted the words of the famous children's hymn:

> Jesus loves me, this I know,
> For the Bible tells me so.

The cross is the symbol of not only God's love in Christ but also Christian discipleship. In five passages, Jesus used the image of the cross to describe a life of sacrifice and self-surrender. For example, in Mark 8 Jesus declared, "If any want to become my followers, let them deny themselves and take up their cross and follow me. For those who want to save their life will lose it, and those who lose their life for my sake, and for the sake of the gospel, will save it. For what will it profit them to gain the whole world and forfeit their life? Indeed, what can they give in return for their life?" (Mark 8:34b–37; cf. Matt. 10:38, 16:24–28; Luke 9:23–26, 14:25–33).

For centuries Christians have been summoned to follow Christ by surrendering themselves and by sacrificing their own desires. They have debated what the cross might mean. Does this mean that a disciple must be prepared to pick up Christ's cross and follow him to the point of death? It did for many early Christians—including Paul—and even in the twentieth century allegiance to Christ has meant suffering, persecution, and death for Christians throughout the world.

Christ's summons to the cross means also the sacrifice of our own desires in obedience to God's call. The Gospel of Mark tells the story of the rich young ruler who asked how to inherit eternal life. Jesus responded by telling him to obey the commandments. The man replied that he had done so since his youth, and then the Gospel says, "Jesus, looked at him, loved him and said, 'You lack one thing; go, sell what you own, and give the money to the poor, and you will have treasure in heaven; then come, follow me.' When he heard this, he was shocked and he went away grieving, for he had many possessions" (Mark 10:21–22).

The cross is used elsewhere in the New Testament as a sign of Christian discipleship. Those who oppose Christ are "enemies of the cross" (for example Phil. 3:18). New life in Christ involves a death to sin and the birth of new life (Rom. 6:4–7). A person who lives in Christ has "crucified the flesh with its passions and desires" to follow the Spirit (Gal. 5:24–26). The letter to the Hebrews suggests one of the most powerful images—the Christian life as a pilgrimage. As pilgrims, we are summoned to "run with perseverance the race that is set before us, looking to Jesus the pioneer and perfecter of our faith, who for the sake of the joy that was set before him endured the cross, disregarding its shame, and has taken his seat at the right hand of the throne of God" (12:1–2).

The cross is therefore both the sign of radical Christian discipleship in suffering for and with Christ as well as the sign of the hope and triumph of the Christian life. As John Calvin declared, "Now we see how many good things, interwoven, spring from the cross. For, overturning that good opinion which we falsely entertain concerning our own strength, and unmasking our hypocrisy, which affords us delight, the cross strikes at our perilous confidence in the flesh. It teaches us, thus humbled, to rest upon God alone, with the result that we do not faint or yield. Hope, moreover, follows victory insofar as the Lord, by performing what he has promised, establishes his truth for the time to come" (*Institutes*, 3. 8. 3).

More than four hundred different versions of the cross have emerged in the history of Christianity. At first the early Protestant Reformers rejected the use of the cross as a symbol of Christianity because they attempted to rid the church of devotion to images. They frowned upon the popular use of crucifixes as a devotional aid in the Roman Catholic tradition; crosses were banned from churches and denounced for personal use. Early Protestants even destroyed crosses in their zeal to "purify" the church. It is estimated that there were 360 public Celtic crosses in Scotland prior to the Reformation; only two exist today.

The cross in the Presbyterian seal is modeled after the Celtic cross that eventually became widely used in the Presbyterian tradition. Sometimes called the Ionic or Irish cross, it is one of the most ancient forms of the cross and was developed by ancient Celtic people in Ireland and Great Britain. A very old and beautiful example can be found on the island of Iona,

13

where the first Irish missionaries began their work in Scotland. Apparently used as a cemetery marker, the Celtic cross usually, but not always, includes a circle or orb that unites the four points of the cross and symbolizes eternity. Because the circle has no beginning or end, it serves as a reminder of the description of God as Alpha–Omega in Revelation 22:13.

If one removes the dove from the Presbyterian seal, the Tau cross appears. This is the oldest known form of the cross and the one most closely associated with the crucifixion. The name is taken from the Greek word for the letter *T*.

The Tau cross is sometimes called the Old Testament cross, the cross of prophecy, the anticipatory cross, or the Mosaic cross. This is based on the reference to Moses lifting up a bronze serpent on a pole. Anyone bitten by a snake could look at the bronze serpent and live (Num. 21:8–9). In the Gospel of John, Jesus declares: "And just as Moses lifted up the serpent in the wilderness, so must the Son of man be lifted up, that whoever believes in him may have eternal life" (3:14–15). Similarly, one tradition suggests that the Hebrews made the sign of the cross on the doors of their houses in Egypt on the night of the Passover (Ex. 12:22).

Thus, the shape of the Presbyterian cross links the Presbyterian Church to two of the oldest symbols of Christianity and recognizes the roots of Christianity in the Old Testament and the people of Israel. It further suggests the abiding message of the cross—the life of forgiveness given to us through God's love.

The cross is the most universal symbol of Christianity and the most ecumenical. Today it is used in various forms by virtually every Christian church. For Protestants, in particular, it points to the heart of Reformation theology: justification by grace through faith. The Second Helvetic Confession summarized this affirmation as follows: "Therefore, because faith receives Christ our righteousness, and attributes everything to the grace of God in Christ, on that account justification is

14

attributed to faith, chiefly because of Christ and not therefore because it is our work. For it is the gift of God" (*Book of Confessions*, Presbyterian Church (U.S.A.), 5.109).

Martin Luther once declared that all theology begins at the foot of the cross. Luther meant that we cannot remove the cross from Christianity without emptying faith of its power and its truth. As the apostle Paul put it, "God proves his love for us in that while we still were sinners Christ died for us. . . . If we live, we live to the Lord, and if we die, we die to the Lord; so then, whether we live or whether we die, we are the Lord's. For to this end Christ died and lived again, so that he might be Lord of both the dead and the living" (Rom. 5:8; 14:8–9).

In the way of the cross is our forgiveness, our life, and our hope: "I have been crucified with Christ; and it is no longer I who live, but it is Christ who lives in me. And the life I now live in the flesh I live by faith in the Son of God, who loved me and gave himself for me" (Gal. 2:19–20).

15

THE DOVE

The figure of a dove, one of the oldest symbols in the history of Christianity, forms the top of the cross. The dove is often shown with a circle or nimbus surrounding its head, indicating that it is holy, but even without the nimbus, the dove symbolizes the presence of God as the Holy Spirit and peace and purity. The meaning of the dove draws on many passages in the Old and New Testaments, but the two most common are the stories of Noah and the flood and the baptism of Jesus.

In the account of Noah and the flood in Genesis 8, the dove symbolizes peace between God and creation. When the waters receded after forty days, Noah first sent out a raven and then a dove. The dove returned to the ark. After waiting seven more days, Noah released the dove again. "And the dove came back to him in the evening, and there in its beak was a freshly plucked olive leaf; so Noah knew that the waters had subsided from the earth" (8:11).

Within this story is found the basis for the dove as the symbol of peace and new life. The enmity between God and the world had ended, and God promised that "as long as the earth endures, seedtime and harvest, cold and heat, summer and winter, day and night, shall not cease" (8:22).

The Christian use of the dove as a symbol of the Holy Spirit is drawn from the story of the baptism of Jesus, found in all four Gospels (Matt. 3:13–17; Mark 1:9–11; Luke 3:21–22; John 1:29–34). As Jesus was being baptized by John the Baptist, a dove descended and a voice was heard from heaven, "This is my Son, the Beloved, with whom I am well pleased" (Matt. 3:17).

For centuries the dove has been one of the most widely used symbols of the Holy Spirit. In Luke and Matthew, the connection is explicit: "The Holy Spirit descended upon him in bodily form like a dove" (Luke 3:22; Matt. 3:16). John's account emphasizes that John the Baptist did not recognize Jesus as the one sent from God. Only when the Holy Spirit came down in the form of a dove did John recognize Christ as the one who would baptize with the Holy Spirit: "And I myself have seen and have testified that this is the Son of God" (John 1:34). The dove as a symbol of the Holy Spirit has always been linked to the sacrament of baptism. In this act, God accepts us as members of a new community, bound by the power of the Spirit.

One of the marks of that community is that through repentance its members have been purged of sin. They are also united in peace with one another and with God. Jesus used the dove to illustrate one part of the challenge of being his disciples when he said, "See, I am sending you out like sheep into the midst of wolves; so be wise as serpents and innocent as doves" (Matt. 10:16).

The dove is also a symbol of sacrifice, in part because of its purity, but also because it was used in ancient Israel as a sacrifice, particularly by the poor. It was used as a substitute for more costly sacrifices and thus connotes both piety and poverty. When Jesus' parents brought two turtledoves to the temple for sacrifice (Luke 2:24), they were following the ancient practice of purification stipulated in Leviticus 12:6–8. Throughout the Old Testament there are many references to doves offered as sacrifices to remove impurity and to make individuals pure before God.

One of the most beautiful images of the dove in the Old Testament comes from the Song of Solomon. There the male poet refers to his beloved: "My dove, my perfect one, [who] is the only one, the darling of her mother, flawless to her that bore her" (6:9). Similarly, the female poet choruses: "His eyes are like doves beside springs of water, bathed in milk, fitly set" (5:12). The basis for the purity and innocence of the dove is rooted in fact, for the dove is purported to be monogamous. The Christian church interpreted the Song of Solomon as a sign of Christ's love for the church, and it drew on the eloquent poetry of this book and the symbol of a dove that has only one object of its love.

At other points in the Old Testament the dove is used in a variety of symbolic ways. The psalmist in distress wanted to escape like a dove and find peace (Ps. 55:6) and knew that the only defense of Israel as a dove against the vultures was the power of God (Ps. 74:19). The iridescent silvery or gold sheen of the dove's feathers symbolizes the presence of God in the cloud that remained with the people of Israel in the wilderness (Ps. 68:13). Occasionally the dove appears as a metaphor for stupidity (Hosea 7:11), but more often it is a sign of strength and purity (Isa. 60:8; Jer. 48:28; Ezek. 7:16).

The Hebrew word for dove literally means "moaner," undoubtedly referring to the bird's call. Isaiah used the image to convey the agony of Hezekiah:

> Like a swallow or a crane I clamor,
> I moan like a dove. (Isa. 38:14)

Isaiah's own distress over the sinfulness of the people is embodied in his lament:

> We all growl like bears;
> like doves we moan mournfully.
> We wait for justice, but there is none;
> for salvation, but it is far from us. (Isa. 59:11)

When Christians began to identify the dove with the Holy Spirit, they relied on the images of the dove from the Hebrew tradition. The pure, innocent bird, who moans when it calls and loves only one mate, provided a powerful way of describing the enduring and consoling presence of the Holy Spirit. It suggested a link to the spirit of God brooding over the waters (Gen. 1:2) and forging the goodness of creation. It also became the sign of what Jesus described as "the Advocate, the Holy Spirit, whom the Father will send in my name, [who] will teach you everything, and remind you of all that I have said to you" (John 14:26).

To a world threatened by nuclear destruction, to a world wracked by violence, to a world devastated by famine and disease, the dove has become a symbol of Christian hope for reconciliation and peace. In the story of Noah and the flood and in the baptism of Jesus, the dove brought a message, and that good news is what we as disciples are commissioned to proclaim to the world. Through the power of the Holy Spirit, descending on the church and strengthening and inspiring the disciples of Christ, Jesus' words become both a source of comfort and a summons to faithful witness: "Peace I leave with you; my peace I give to you. I do not give to you as the world gives" (John 14:27).

Centuries later, the dove as the Holy Spirit calls us to be agents of the reconciliation of the world—its peace and wholeness. In the words of the Confession of 1967, "God the Holy Spirit fulfills the work of reconciliation in humanity. The Holy Spirit creates and renews the church as the community in which people are reconciled to God and to one another. God enables them to receive forgiveness as they forgive one another and to enjoy the peace of God as they make peace among themselves. In spite of their sin, God gives them power to become representatives of Jesus Christ and his gospel of reconciliation to all people" (*Book of Confessions,* 9.20, alt.).

THE FISH

One of the little-noticed symbols in the Presbyterian seal is the image of a fish. It can be seen by mentally removing the wings of the dove. The asymmetrical body of the dove then becomes a fish. The hidden quality of the fish is appropriate, for the fish was used by early Christians as a secret sign that both disguised and revealed their identities as followers of Christ.

The fish was the earliest symbol of secret Christian self-identification, first used during the persecution of the early Christians as a code for believers. The carved symbol of a fish might be worn around the neck. A believer might draw the outline of a fish in the dust, or during conversation a person might draw only half of the fish, leaving it to the other person to complete. As early as the late second century, Clement of Alexandria recommended using the fish on seals and rings with no explanation of its meaning, which suggests that the use of the fish as a Christian sign was already widespread. The fish also is found frequently on the walls and tombs of the early catacombs.

Why and how the fish became a symbol of Christianity so quickly is wrapped in the same mystery that surrounded its use. For the most part, the biblical writers make infrequent figurative use of them. One of the most striking images of a fish as new life is found in Ezekiel's description of the river that will flow from the Temple to the Dead Sea so that fish will multiply there (47:7–10). In the apocryphal book of Tobit, Tobias ate a fish that protected him from evil (ch. 6). In the book of Jonah, the great fish saved Jonah and then after three days spewed him out so he could fulfill his prophetic calling. The early church drew a parallel between the three days of suffering for Jonah and Christ's lying in the tomb, and thus the sign of Jonah appears frequently in the catacombs.

References to fish also appear in the Gospels, sometimes referring to people. Jesus likened the kingdom of heaven to a net gathering many different fish; the good ones were saved, the bad were cast away (Matt. 13:47–50). Jesus called fishermen to be his disciples, telling them they would become fishers of men and women (Matt. 4:18–21; Mark 1:16–17; Luke 5:1–11).

But the Gospel of John also contains a story of fish that conveys what the early church eventually interpreted as the meaning of the fish as a symbol. It not only depicted those who followed Christ but also Christ himself. In John 21, Jesus appeared to the disciples early in the morning after his resurrection. He told them to bring some of the fish they had just caught, and Simon Peter brought the net, filled with 153 large fish. The disciples recognized Jesus, and after cooking the fish he gave them bread and fish (21:9–14).

One theory holds that people then believed there were 153 species of fish in the world, and that John's reference to the quantity was his way of symbolically suggesting the universal character of the gospel of Jesus Christ. More important, the fish revealed Christ to his disciples in a sacramental meal (see also Matt. 14:17ff., 15:34ff.; Mark 6:38ff.; 8:7ff.; Luke 9:13ff.; 24:42; John 6:9ff.).

The fish probably became such a widespread symbol of both Christ and his followers because of Jesus' call to fishermen to be his disciples. Equally significant was the early church's emphasis on baptism, especially of adults. Jesus was first revealed as the Christ at the moment of his baptism. As one historian put it, Jesus was God revealed in the water. Christians, who are baptized in Christ's name, thus become fish like Christ and swim in the water that he has purified. They also eat fish, which God has provided for those who belong to the kingdom, and they receive new life. Tertullian, writing around the year A.D. 200, said, "But we, little fishes, after the example of our FISH Jesus Christ, are born in the water." By the word "fish," Augustine declared, "Christ is mystically understood because he was able to live, that is, to exist without sin in the abyss of this mortality as in the depth of waters." In other words, the fish became an inclusive symbol for many dimensions of the church's faith—Jesus Christ, his followers, baptism, resurrection, the Lord's Supper, and the kingdom of God.

Probably by later coincidence, the Greek word for fish (*ichthys*) was seen as an acronym for "Jesus, Son of God, Savior." The first letter of each of the Greek words—*Iesous Christos, Theou Huios, Soter*—spelled *ichthys,* or fish. The early Christians thus had a mysterious sign that conveyed their faith and their own identity as people who had been baptized with water in the name of Christ, the fish who saved others.

The fish as a symbol has not been widely used in recent Christian art, but it is fitting that the Presbyterian seal recovers this ancient sign. The symbol arose in the midst of the church facing adversity and persecution. Although American Presbyterians are spared outright hostility to their faith, the church does confront a culture that is resistant or apathetic to the call of Christ to be disciples. In other parts of the world, the church suffers from actual persecution. The sign of the fish gives to all Christians a reminder of the cost of discipleship.

That summons is beautifully illustrated in the well-known story of Jesus' feeding the five thousand with five loaves and two fish. The account appears in all four Gospels with one common theme. The disciples could not believe that Jesus, who had compassion on the hungry crowd, wanted to feed everyone. In Mark's version, the disciples sarcastically asked Jesus, "Are we to go and buy two hundred denarii worth of bread, and give it to them to eat?" (6:37), knowing full well they did not have anything like that amount of money. But Jesus took the five loaves and two fish and blessed them. Then the food was distributed to the crowd, "and all ate and were filled" (6:42). Twelve baskets of leftover bread and fish remained (Matt. 14:13–21; Mark 6:30–44; Luke 9:10–17; John 6:1–14).

The story of the feeding of the five thousand warns us about the shallowness of a faith that relies upon human calculations of what is possible. It provides also a reminder of God's calling to us to be concerned about the welfare of others. Christ's compassion for the hungry five thousand prompted him to ask the disciples for food. His love for the people created the miracle of five loaves and two fish multiplying to feed the crowd. The good news of the Christian faith calls American Presbyterians who have so much of the world's wealth to have compassion on those who hunger, those who are poor, and those who thirst for new life. Through the power of God in Christ, we are called to be fishers who will let down nets that bring in all the people of God to a banquet where no one will hunger again.

Standing at the center of the victory over sin and evil is Jesus Christ. As stated in "A Declaration of Faith" (*Our Confessional Heritage*, 1978):

> All things will be renewed in Christ. . . .
>
> As he stands at the center of our history,
>> we are confident he will stand at its end.
> He will judge all people and nations.
> Evil will be condemned
>> and rooted out of God's good creation.
> There will be no more tears or pain.
> All things will be made new.
> The fellowship of human beings with God and each other
>> will be perfected.

THE BOOK

Protestants are people of the book—the Bible. "Sola Scriptura"—Latin for "scripture alone"—was one of the great rallying cries of all branches of the Protestant Reformation. The churches of the Calvinist or Reformed family of Protestantism have likewise made scripture the supreme authority for Christian faith and life. In the words of the Westminster Larger Catechism (*Book of Confessions*, 7.113), the Bible is "the only rule of faith and obedience."

It is not surprising that when Presbyterian and Reformed churches began to develop symbols and seals, a book or the Bible was frequently depicted. For example, in the seal of the former Presbyterian Church in the U.S., the Bible appears as an open-faced book with "The Word of God" printed on one page and a serpent intertwined around a cross on the other. References to two biblical texts are at the top of each page—1 Peter 1:23 ("You have been born anew, not of perishable but of imperishable seed, through the living and enduring word of God") and John 3:14 ("And just as Moses lifted up the serpent in the wilderness, so must the Son of Man be lifted up"). Similarly, the seal of the former United Presbyterian Church in the U.S.A. contains a book with an alpha and an omega on the open pages. Through the book is an arrow with an alpha tip and an omega end, symbolizing the power of the Word of God to penetrate the sinful heart.

In making the Bible the authority for the Christian life, Luther and Calvin protested the Roman Catholic position that scripture *and* the tradition of the church wielded equal authority and some "radicals'" or Anabaptists' position that direct instruction from the Holy Spirit was paramount in the life of the church. The only source of our knowledge of God and our salvation in Jesus Christ, they proclaimed, comes from scripture and scripture alone. As Calvin declared, "Scripture, gathering up the otherwise confused knowledge of God in our minds, having dispersed our dullness, clearly shows us the true God" (Institutes, 1.6.1).

The emphasis on the authority of the Bible had its own pitfalls, and the history of the Calvinist tradition is marked by many debates about the meaning of biblical authority. One line of argument made the Bible authoritative because it was inspired by God and therefore infallible. Particularly in reaction to modern biblical scholarship, this argument hardened into an insistence on an inspired, inerrant text of the Bible—at least as it was found in the original manuscripts.

Lost in this debate was a theme sounded by both Luther and Calvin. For these Reformers, the Bible had authority because it teaches us the saving work of Jesus Christ. Our knowledge of God's grace in the Bible comes through the life and work of countless missionaries and preachers and a great cloud of witnesses throughout the centuries. The authority of scripture rests upon Jesus Christ and the work of the Holy Spirit in making scripture the Word of God. As Calvin maintained, "For even if [Scripture] wins reverence for itself by its own majesty, it seriously affects us only when it is sealed upon our hearts through the Spirit" (Institutes, 1.7.5). The placement of the dove directly above the open Bible was intended to signify the important role of the Holy Spirit in both inspiring scripture and interpreting the words of scripture as God's word to us.

This emphasis on scripture was not something new that the Reformers invented in the sixteenth century; rather, it lies at the heart of the Bible itself. In the Old Testament, the Torah is God's word to the people of Israel. The law, given to Moses, explained God's ordering of human life so that people might remain in communion with God. The covenant with Israel was based on God's love and the faithfulness of the people to the Word of God. When the people were unfaithful, it was because they had forsaken the covenant or forgotten its provisions. The reforms of King Josiah and Nehemiah recover the importance of the law, for this was God's word to them (2 Kings 23; 2 Chron. 34; Neh. 8). The psalmists also focused on a reverence for God's word in the law. For example, Psalm 1 praises those whose "delight is in the law of the LORD, and on his law they meditate day and night" (v. 2). Psalm 119 is an extended hymn to God for the majesty of the law and the blessing of God's word:

> I treasure your word in my heart,
>   so that I may not sin against you (v. 11).
>
> Your word is a lamp to my feet
>   and a light to my path (v. 105).

In the eyes of the prophets, the people of Israel have been punished because they have rejected the covenant and remained deaf to the word of God.

One of the central themes of the New Testament is the affirmation that Jesus is the Word of God incarnate. Christ fulfills scripture. John's Gospel opens with the declaration: "In the beginning was the Word, and the Word was with God, and the Word was God. . . . And the Word became flesh and lived among us . . . full of grace and truth" (1:1, 14).

When Jesus began his ministry in Nazareth, according to Luke, he went to the synagogue, read from the prophet Isaiah, and then declared, "Today this scripture has been fulfilled in your hearing" (Luke 4:16–21). According to the Gospel writers, Christ's miracles, teaching, persecution, death, and resurrection were all designed to fulfill the words of scripture. And when Jesus appeared to the disciples on the road to Emmaus and later to the gathered disciples, he explained the events of his death and resurrection by opening "their minds to understand the scriptures" (Luke 24:13–45).

31

Similarly, the disciples relied on scripture to explain the meaning of Christ's life and teaching. Philip evangelized the Ethiopian eunuch by explaining the scriptures (Acts 8:26–40); Paul went to Thessalonica, and "on three sabbath days argued with them from the scriptures, explaining and proving that it was necessary for the Messiah to suffer and to rise from the dead" (Acts 17:2–3). Paul's letters, particularly the letter to the Romans, were extended expositions of how God's Word had been fulfilled in Jesus Christ and how the words of scripture had been realized in the death and resurrection of Jesus. Paul summarized his attempt to preach the gospel based on scripture in the letter to the church at Corinth: "For I handed on to you as of first importance what I in turn had received: that Christ died for our sins in accordance with the scriptures, and that he was buried, and that he was raised on the third day in accordance with the scriptures, and that he appeared to Cephas, then to the twelve" (1 Cor. 15:3–5). And in an apocalyptic vision, John described a "book of life" which will bring judgment upon the sin of the world and offer salvation to all who believe in Christ (Rev. 3:5–7, 5:1–14, 13:8–10, 17:8, 20:12–15).

The Bible as the Word of God in the law and in the grace of Jesus Christ pervades Calvinist theology. A distinguishing mark of Calvin's theology is often called Calvin's third use of the law. The first use of the law was to convict individuals of their sin, and the second was to provide them with a pattern for the moral life. But Calvin insisted on a third use, which was more inclusive and corporate. The law, he argued, could become the very structure of grace in the world. Properly understood and enforced, the law and the institutions of society and government could become ways of achieving God's will in human affairs (*Institutes*, 2.7). Many historians see in this third use the basis for the Calvinist impulse to transform society and reform its institutions, and the history of Calvinism in America and other countries is noteworthy because of

Calvinist political activism and social concern—rooted in the authority of scripture.

This elevation of God's Word above all human words, this declaration that divine law is superior to all human laws, was the theological foundation for the Theological Declaration of Barmen issued by the Confessing Church in Germany in protest against Hitler: "We reject the false doctrine, as though the State, over and beyond its special commission, should and could become the single and totalitarian order of human life, thus fulfilling the Church's vocation as well" *(Book of Confessions,* 8.23). The same spirit animates the Reformed protest against apartheid in South Africa. These Calvinists believe that apartheid is "a heresy," for in making dark-skinned people inferior to whites, it fundamentally contradicts the Word of God in the Bible.

The Bible of the Presbyterian seal is an open book, symbolizing its accessibility to all the people of God. The priesthood of all believers—a doctrine shared by all Protestants—does not attempt to deny the authority of priests, but affirms the common calling of all Christians to respond to God's love in Jesus Christ. Through the open Bible, all are invited to receive the forgiveness of God in Christ and to learn the law of the Lord. In studying the Bible we are guided by the Holy Spirit, which will show us anew the power of God's grace in Jesus Christ and who will equip us for ministry in Christ's name.

During the last two hundred years, with the rise of the modern Christian missionary movement, the open Bible has symbolized also the translation of scripture into thousands of languages and dialects. This remarkable development has now made it possible to read and hear the Word of God in the words of millions of people throughout the world.

The authority of the Bible is central to what it means to be Presbyterian and to share in the Protestant tradition. It is an idea that had revolutionary consequences at the time of the Reformation, and it continues to raise troubling questions

33

about the authorities accepted in our modern world. Protestants have sometimes been tempted to use the Bible as a book with near magical qualities. They have also been accused of making the Bible into a "paper pope" or of bibliolatry—worshiping the Bible rather than the God who became flesh in Jesus Christ and is revealed in the Bible. Today people are more apt to treat the Bible as an icon—the least-read best-seller in America. But the centrality and authority of the Bible for our lives cannot be escaped by a false reverence for scripture or by quietly ignoring its claims on our lives; as 2 Timothy declares, "All scripture is inspired by God and is useful for teaching, for reproof, for correction, and for training in righteousness, so that everyone who belongs to God may be proficient, equipped for every good work" (3:16–17).

THE PULPIT

The Bible of the Presbyterian seal lies on a pulpit or lectern, symbolizing the importance of preaching in the Presbyterian tradition. Presbyterians shared with other Protestants an emphasis on the sermon, preached to congregations as the word of God. The historian, James Hastings Nichols, has argued that the renewed significance of the sermon during the sixteenth century constituted a revolution in Christian worship.

Today it may be hard to appreciate why the sermon became so important and popular since preaching is important in all branches of Christianity. However, when the Reformation began, the central act of Christian worship was the celebration of the Mass, a sacramental act in which the people observed the priest, partook of only the bread, and listened to Latin words that few understood. The Reformers restored preaching to worship—a sermon based on scripture. Just as the Bible was translated into the language of the people, so also the exposition of scripture in worship was communicated in their own language. Particularly in Puritanism, preachers strove to proclaim the truth of Christianity in plain and simple language. In a sense, the sermon both stimulated and responded to a populist and democratic impulse in Protestant Christianity.

In American Presbyterianism, the zeal for preaching reached an extreme. From the seventeenth through the nineteenth centuries, worship became little else than the proclamation of the Word—sometimes for two or three hours—plus the delivery of very long prayers by the minister. At first only Psalms were allowed to be sung, but gradually the hymns of Isaac Watts, the Wesleys, and others were accepted. Finally, in the twentieth century, Presbyterians rediscovered the richness of sixteenth-century worship and liturgy in Calvin's Geneva and other centers of Reformed life. But the fact remains that Presbyterians continue to place a very high value on preaching. Many still see the reading of scripture and the sermon as the heart of Christian worship.

Although the sermon did revolutionize Christian worship in the sixteenth century, the Protestant Reformers did not see themselves as doing anything new. On the contrary, they sought to recapture the church of the New Testament, and here they had ample biblical warrant for the importance of preaching. They read the Gospels and saw that preaching was central to Christ's ministry. For example, when Jesus began his ministry in Nazareth, he read a passage from the book of Isaiah that seemed to embody his call to proclaim the kingdom of God:

> The Spirit of the Lord is upon me,
> because he has anointed me
> to bring good news to the poor.
>
> He has sent me to proclaim release to the captives
> and recovery of sight to the blind,
> to let the oppressed go free,
> to proclaim the year of our Lord's favor.
> (Luke 4:18–19; cf. Isa. 61:1–2)

In this act and with the announcement that "today this scripture has been fulfilled in your hearing," Jesus linked himself with the tradition of the prophets who proclaimed the word of God and identified himself as the one chosen by God to initiate the reign of God.

The terms "preach" and "preaching" do not appear often in the Old Testament and usually are associated with the prophets or "the Preacher" of Ecclesiastes. But the terms are widely used in the New Testament. Here the Christian understanding of preaching as the proclamation of the gospel took root. Biblical scholars agree that the fundamental content of that proclamation included these central themes. The message of the gospel is the good news that God has become human in Jesus Christ and has inaugurated a new reign in human history. The kingdom of God is a judgment on people for their sin. If they are moved to repentance, they will be restored to God through the death and resurrection of Jesus Christ. In Christ, people have new life. In turn God commissions them to proclaim the good news to others. (See, for example, Peter's sermon in Acts 10:36–43.)

Christ recognized that the evil of the world would make it impossible for some to hear the gospel—a powerful theme in the Gospel of John. Jesus warned his disciples about the difficulties they would confront as heralds of the kingdom (Mark 6:7–13; Luke 9:1–6). Paul acknowledged that preaching Christ as crucified was "a stumbling block to Jews and foolishness to Gentiles, but to those who are called, both Jews and Greeks," Christ becomes "the power of God and the wisdom of God" (1 Cor. 1:23–24). Paul also referred repeatedly to his suffering for the sake of the gospel (2 Cor. 11:23–28), and the second letter to Timothy identifies suffering with the calling to be a disciple and a preacher:

> Do not be ashamed, then, of the testimony about our Lord, or of me his prisoner, but join with me in suffering for the gospel, relying on the power of God, who saved us and called us with a holy calling, not according to our works but according to his own purpose and grace. This grace was given to us in Christ Jesus before the ages began, but it has now been revealed through the appearing of our Savior Christ Jesus, who abolished death and brought life and immortality to light through the gospel. For this gospel I was appointed a herald and an apostle and a teacher, and for this reason I suffer as I do (1:8–12a).

Throughout the New Testament the primary affirmation is that the gospel is Jesus Christ, and the preaching of the

39

gospel is God's revelation in Jesus Christ. The person proclaiming the gospel seemed to be irrelevant to whether the gospel was true (Phil. 1:15–18); as Paul wrote to the church at Corinth, "For we do not proclaim ourselves; we proclaim Jesus Christ as Lord and ourselves as your slaves for Jesus' sake" (2 Cor. 4:5).

Some biblical scholars argue for a clear delineation between the preaching and teaching of Jesus. When Jesus preached, he was proclaiming the gospel to those who did not believe, and his teaching was reserved for his disciples. Others insist that this division is too rigid, for the teaching and preaching of Jesus were intertwined.

In the Presbyterian tradition, the office of pastor has always been understood as embracing both preaching and teaching. At one point in our history, pastors were given the title "teaching elders," in contrast to elders who were "ruling elders." The terminology is not as widely used today, but it does demonstrate the importance of education in the Presbyterian tradition.

The open book on a lectern in the Presbyterian seal might also be interpreted as a symbol of the educational emphasis that has been such a prominent part of the Presbyterian tradition. From Calvin's Genevan academy to the present, the Calvinist movement has been one that recognized, in Calvin's words, that "ignorance is a curse upon the church."

The Reformers' emphasis on the knowledge of the Bible and the translation of the Bible into the language of the people contributed to an extraordinary explosion of literacy in the Western world. The growth of literacy was especially prominent in areas where Calvinism was strong. By the time of the American Revolution, 90 percent of the men and 50 percent of the women in New England knew how to read and write, a percentage far higher than in any area of Europe.

In America, Calvinists quickly established common schools for children, colleges, and eventually seminaries. Presbyterians founded such major universities as Princeton, the University of North Carolina, and the University of Tennessee. In Presbyterian missionary activity, there was the same educational impulse, for a school was often constructed as soon as the church building was completed.

The open book on the pulpit beneath a descending dove is a symbol of the Presbyterian tradition's dual emphases on preaching and teaching, guided and informed by the Holy Spirit. That tradition recognizes both the challenge to conserve the heritage of the past and the summons to teach and proclaim the wisdom and power of God in a new era. In the words of Paul to the church at Rome: "But how are they to call on one in whom they have not believed? And how are they to believe in one of whom they have never heard? And how are they to hear without someone to proclaim him? And how are they to proclaim him unless they are sent? As it is written, 'How beautiful are the feet of those who bring good news!'" (Rom. 10:14–15).

THE CUP

One of the most creative features of the Presbyterian seal is the cup. It can be seen by looking at the spine of the book and mentally removing the covers of the book at each side so that the half circle remains. The cup is supported by the central horizontal line of the cross and by the base of the cross. The cup thus becomes both a chalice and a baptismal font, symbols of the two sacraments—baptism and the Lord's Supper.

Notice the location of the cup (chalice, or baptismal font). Integrated into the design of the book, it symbolizes the Reformed emphasis on the relationship between Word and sacrament. Placed within the cross, it symbolizes the basic Christian affirmation that the sacraments are visible signs of God's grace in Jesus Christ given to the church. Located beneath the dove, it symbolizes the importance of the Holy Spirit in making baptism and the Lord's Supper the means of grace for the individual. Finally, there is an implied triangle formed by the sides of the flames and the base of the cross. The triangle serves as a symbol for the Trinity, and the peak of the triangle intersects with the center of the cup. This recognizes that both the Lord's Supper and baptism are celebrated in the name of the Father, the Son, and the Holy Spirit.

In the Bible, the cup refers to either a drinking vessel or a portion provided. Its connotations are both positive and negative. For example, there is the familiar reference in Psalm 23: "You anoint my head with oil; my cup overflows" (v. 5). In Psalm 116, the psalmist declared, "I will lift up the cup of salvation and call on the name of the LORD" (v. 13), and Jeremiah referred to "the cup of consolation" provided by God (16:7). But the cup also could be a vessel of God's judgment. Psalm 75 contains the dramatic image of a cup of "foaming wine," which the Lord will pour out and "all the wicked of the earth shall drain it down to the dregs" (v. 8). Jeremiah described Babylon as a golden cup in the Lord's hand, out of which all the nations drank and went mad (51:7). In Revelation there are also many references to the cup of the wrath of God (14:10, 16:19, 17:4, 18:6).

The symbolism of the cup was powerfully associated with Jesus himself and therefore has a distinctive Christian meaning. Above all, it embodies the idea of Christ's suffering, death, and resurrection—the pouring out of his life as a sacrifice for the salvation of the world. In Gethsemane, Jesus fell on his face and prayed, "My Father, if it is possible, let this cup pass from me; yet not what I want but what you want" (Matt. 26:39; Mark 14:35–36; Luke 22:41–42). Jesus also referred to his suffering by asking his disciples whether they were able to drink of his cup (Matt. 20:20–23; Mark 10:35–40; John 18:11).

The cup of Christ's suffering was linked to the sacrament of the Lord's Supper in the accounts of the Last Supper. There, Jesus assembled his disciples, gave thanks for the wine and bread, and declared, "Drink from it, all of you; for this is my blood of the covenant, which is poured out for many for the forgiveness of sins. I tell you, I will never again drink of this fruit of the vine until that day when I drink it new with you in my Father's kingdom" (Matt. 26:26–29; cf. Mark 14:22–25; Luke 22:14–23).

The familiar "words of institution" of the Lord's Supper from Paul's first letter to the Corinthians unite the image of the cup with Christ's suffering even more directly: "For I received from the Lord what I also handed on to you, that the Lord Jesus on the night when he was betrayed took a loaf of bread, and when he had given thanks, he broke it and said, 'This is my body that is for you. Do this in remembrance of me.' In the same way he took the cup also, after supper, saying, 'This cup is the new covenant in my blood. Do this, as often as you drink it, in remembrance of me.' For as often as you eat this bread and drink this cup, you proclaim the Lord's death until he comes" (11:23–26).

The Lord's Supper soon became the center of the early church's worship. Its origins are complex, but it was undoubtedly connected to the celebration of Passover. Very quickly it became a eucharistic meal, in which Christians both recalled the death and resurrection of Christ and were made one with Christ and one another. At first there was no formal doctrine or theory of the Lord's Supper, but soon debate arose over how the sacrament should be celebrated and the meaning of the sacrament itself. That debate has continued to the present day. Many have noted the terrible irony that even though the Lord's Supper is supposed to unify Christians, it is around the table that the various Christian traditions are most divided.

Luther's and Calvin's basic protests against the Catholic Mass were centered in their refusal to accept the Mass as a reenactment of the sacrificial death of Jesus Christ. That divine act, they argued, had happened once and for all. Although Luther and Calvin disagreed about what the Lord's Supper did mean, and differed from other Reformers such as Zwingli, the Reformers were united in three affirmations about the sacrament.

First, in the Lord's Supper, participants are united with Christ. In repentance, people who partake of the bread and the wine are forgiven and restored to union with God. The broken bread and Christ's broken body transform the shattered lives of people and make them whole. The poured wine and the blood shed are a transfusion of new and cleansed blood that brings new life.

Second, believers are united with each other. They become one body—the body of Christ (Rom. 12; 1 Cor. 12). As they eat the bread and drink the wine, they are bonded to one another by the Christ who died and rose again that the world and its people might be saved from one another and for one another. Using the familiar imagery of the body of Christ, Calvin summarized the dual union with God and others in this way:

> For the Lord so communicates his body to us there that he is made completely one with us and we with him. Now, since he has only one body, of which he makes us all partakers, it is necessary that all of us also be made one body by such participation. The bread shown in the Sacrament represents this unity. As it is made of many grains so mixed together that one cannot be distinguished from another, so it is fitting that in the same way we should be joined and bound together by such great agreement of minds that no sort of disagreement or division may intrude. (*Institutes*, 4.17.38)

As Robert McAfee Brown has suggested in his book, *The Spirit of Protestantism*, this idea of the Lord's Supper has "arresting consequences" (p. 154) for Christian ethical responsibility. Calvin wrote that if we accept the bread and the wine, then no one "can be injured, despised, rejected, abused, or in any way offended by us, without at the same time, injuring, despising, and abusing Christ by the wrongs we do" (*Institutes*, 4.17.38).

Third, the Lord's Supper demonstrates not only what God has done in Jesus Christ and what we do in receiving Christ but also the reality of what God intends life to be. Amidst all the fear and violence of this world, amidst all the hatred of ourselves and of others, the Lord's Supper reminds us—visibly— of a God who loved the world so much that Christ became human, suffered, and died, and was raised again so that we could have new life. It is a new life created in a world that demeans life. In taking the simple elements of bread and wine, we can see a different world in which life will triumph over death and love will prevail over fear. In the words of Revelation, God will dwell with the faithful and "will wipe every tear from their eyes. Death will be no more; mourning and crying and pain will be no more, for the first things have passed away" (21:4). The Lord's Supper not only calls people to remember in the past what God has done in Christ but also propels Christians to anticipate in the future the reality God will bring.

The cup symbolizes the sacrament of baptism. The origins of Christian baptism come from the common practice in the ancient Near East of using water for ritual purification. The New Testament describes the ministry of John the Baptist, who preached a baptism of repentance for the forgiveness of sins and proclaimed that one would follow him who would baptize not only with water but with the Holy Spirit (Matt. 3; Mark 1; Luke 3; cf. John 1). John the Baptist baptized Jesus; after came the divine announcement concerning Jesus: "You are my Son the Beloved; with you I am well pleased" (Mark 1:11). The baptism of Jesus thus marked a revelation from God and the beginning of his ministry.

Jesus drew a parallel between his baptism and his "cup of suffering." When James and John asked Jesus for favored places in his kingdom, he replied, "You do not know what you are asking. Are you able to drink the cup that I drink, or be baptized with the baptism that I am baptized with?" (Mark 10:38). Jesus linked his baptism to his suffering and death, a passage from one life to another. The early church took this dual understanding of baptism from the Gospels themselves. Baptism was both the initiation into the fellowship of the church and the beginning of one's ministry. It also began the Christian's migration from a former life of sin to a new life in God's grace.

Four passages from Paul illustrate this understanding of baptism. In 1 Corinthians 12:12–13, Paul taught that even though the body has many members, "in the one Spirit we were all baptized into one body—Jews or Greeks, slaves or free—and we were all made to drink of one Spirit." In

47

Galatians 3:26–29, Paul declared that those who are "baptized into Christ have clothed yourselves with Christ," and offered the same startling conclusion: "There is no longer Jew or Greek, there is no longer slave or free, there is no longer male and female; for all of you are one in Christ Jesus."

In Romans 6:1–6, Paul reminded the believers at Rome of the importance of their baptism, in which they "have been buried with him by baptism into death." Paul's imagery implies a baptism by immersion, and he concluded that just as they emerged from the water, so also they will "walk in newness of life." "For if we have been united with him in a death like his, we will certainly be united with him in a resurrection like his. We know that our old self was crucified with him so that the body of sin might be destroyed, and we might no longer be enslaved to sin." Colossians 2:9–13 makes the same point, arguing that baptism is the counterpart to circumcision and that in baptism the believer becomes dead to sin and alive in Christ.

In the Gospels, it seems obvious that the connection between the proclamation of the gospel and the baptism of believers was inherent in Jesus' message: "All authority in heaven and on earth has been given to me. Go therefore and make disciples of all nations, baptizing them in the name of the Father and of the Son and of the Holy Spirit, and teaching them to obey everything that I have commanded you; and remember, I am with you always, to the end of the age" (Matt. 28:18–20).

The basis for believing that the early church's preaching was related to the practice of baptism comes from the book of Acts. For example, at Pentecost, "those who welcomed" Peter's preaching were baptized (2:37–42). Ananias baptized Paul (9:1–19); Philip's trip to Samaria resulted in many baptisms, "both men and women" (8:12), and he baptized the Ethiopian eunuch (8:36); Peter baptized Cornelius and the members of his household (ch. 10); and Paul baptized new converts at Philippi and Ephesus (chs. 16, 18, 19).

The evidence about the early practice of baptism is slight, but at least this much seems clear. The earliest baptisms were done "in the name of Jesus," and the full use of the trinitarian formula ("in the name of the Father, and of the Son, and of the Holy Spirit") came somewhat later. Baptism of both children and adults was practiced. The most common form of baptism was apparently immersion of the entire body, but pouring water over the convert was also common. Later came the practice of sprinkling. Baptism was administered by pastors and bishops but also by lay leaders.

In the New Testament and in the history of the church, baptism has been a sacrament with multiple layers of meaning. It is the cleansing of sin, a new birth in Christ through the power of the Holy Spirit, union with Christ, and initiation into the fellowship of the church—the body of Christ. One can sense the cycle of passage from repentance to redemption, to new life in community, by imagining the ancient practice of baptism. The believer may have been led to the edge of a large pool. After shedding outer clothes (the old self), the person entered the water. Then came the words of blessing: "I baptize you in the name of the Father, and of the Son, and of the Holy Spirit." The person then emerged from the pool, was given a clean robe, joined the other believers, and was greeted into the fellowship of the church.

The Reformers insisted that baptism, like the Lord's Supper, became effective only when God had awakened faith in the life of the believer, while the Roman Catholic tradition held that the sacrament was valid if rightly performed. This emphasis on the primacy of faith has led some Protestants to reject infant baptism, since infants are not old enough to have a mature understanding of faith. The Presbyterian Church (U.S.A.) recognizes both infant and adult baptism. The theological basis for our practice is the affirmation that in baptism, it is not the act of the individual being baptized but the act of God performed through the church—the community of faith. In baptism we do not decide to join the church, but God bonds us in Christ to one another. God initiates this covenant, as it is often called, and nothing captures our inability and God's ability so clearly than the baptism of an infant. The baptismal service of the French Reformed Church includes this eloquent passage:

> Little child, for you Jesus Christ came into the world, he did battle in the world, he suffered; for you he went through the agony of Gethsemane and the darkness of Calvary; for you he cried, "It is fulfilled"; for you he triumphed over death . . . For you, and you, little child, do not yet know anything about this. But thus is the statement of the apostle confirmed, "We loved God because he first loved us."
> (Robert McAfee Brown, 149)

We will never be able to understand fully the ultimate mystery of the sacraments, just as we will never be able to understand the mystery of a God who loved us while we were yet sinners. In Augustine's famous phrase, sacraments are visible signs of invisible grace. Or, as Calvin declared, a sacrament is "an outward sign by which the Lord seals on our consciences the promises of his good will toward us in order to sustain the weakness of our faith; and we in turn attest our piety toward him in the presence of the Lord and of his angels and before [humanity]" *(Institutes, 4.14.1)*. They are the church's means of conveying God's word of love in Jesus Christ through the power of the Holy Spirit.

This is why the sacraments are always linked to the preaching of the Word. The Presbyterian seal places the symbol of baptism and the Lord's Supper at the heart of the cross (Christ's love), at the center of the book (the Bible), within the pulpit (preaching), beneath the dove (the Holy Spirit), and at the peak of the triangle (the Trinity). As Calvin put it, "For first, the Lord teaches and instructs us by his Word. Secondly, he confirms it by the sacraments. Finally, he illumines our minds by the light of his Holy Spirit and opens our hearts for the Word and sacraments to enter in, which would otherwise only strike our ears and appear before our eyes, but not at all affect us within" (*Institutes*, 4.14.8).

Through the Word and the sacraments, we are sealed in Christ.

THE FIRE

The four flames at the base of the Presbyterian seal draw on many biblical images of fire and light. The meaning of fire is ambiguous, as is fire itself. Since fire is a source of both creativity and destruction, it has a primal power that has fascinated people since the beginning of time. It therefore appears in diverse cultures and various religions as an image for the divine.

The two most familiar biblical references to fire are the burning bush in the Old Testament and the tongues of fire that descended at Pentecost. The story of the burning bush contains many central affirmations of biblical faith that have been emphasized in the Presbyterian tradition, and the burning bush has been a common symbol in other Presbyterian and Reformed symbols, including the seal of the former Presbyterian Church in the U.S.

In Exodus 3, Moses confronted a flame within a bush that is not consumed and turned aside to see "this amazing sight." From the bush God called to Moses and told him to remove his shoes because he was standing on holy ground. And God declared to Moses, " 'I am the God of your father, the God of Abraham, the God of Isaac, and the God of Jacob.' And Moses hid his face, for he was afraid to look at God" (v. 6). Then God declared his intention to deliver the people of Israel from Egypt and to make Moses the leader of the people. Moses protested, "Who am I that I should go to Pharaoh, and bring the Israelites out of Egypt?" And God replied, "I will be with you; and this shall be the sign for you that it is I who sent you: when you have brought the people out of Egypt, you shall worship God on this mountain" (vs. 11–12). But Moses persisted and asked God to tell him who God is, and God replied, "I AM WHO I AM. . . . Thus you shall say to the Israelites, 'I AM has sent me to you'" (vs. 13–14). The passage concludes with God's reminder of his covenant with Abraham and the promise to be the God of the people and deliver them from bondage (vs. 15–22).

The fire in the burning bush is obviously a symbol for God. It is a theophany—a revelation of God—to Moses. But it is a fire that does not consume the bush, suggesting that the God revealed in the bush is merciful and does not destroy. God in the fire is also an awesome God, not to be approached casually. God's presence sanctifies the ground, and Moses must remove his shoes. Moses is awestricken and cannot look at the bush, for no one who sees God will live (Deut. 18:16). And yet God in the fire is also the God who commissions Moses for leadership and reminds him of the promise to be with him and to liberate the people of Israel from Egypt.

The biblical image of the God of the burning bush has often been described in the Calvinist tradition in terms of the sovereignty of God. God is ultimately a mystery, a power above all earthly power, "Wholly Other," to use the famous phrase of Rudolph Otto. We stand in the presence of the holiness of God with reverence and wonder. The seventeenth-century language of the Westminster Confession of Faith may seem archaic or even extreme, but in extolling the majesty of God, the Confession reminds us of a Bach fugue:

> God hath all life, glory, goodness, blessedness, in and of himself; and is alone in and unto himself all-sufficient, not standing in need of any creatures which he hath made, nor deriving any glory from them, but only manifesting his own glory in, by, unto, and upon them: he is alone fountain of all being, of whom, through whom, and to whom, are all things; and hath most sovereign dominion over them, to do by them, for them, or upon them, whatsoever himself pleaseth. In his sight all things are open and manifest; his knowledge is infinite, infallible, and independent upon the creature; so as nothing is to him contingent or uncertain. He is most holy in all his

counsels, in all his works, and in all his commands. To him is due from angels and [people], and every other creature, whatsoever worship, service, or obedience he is pleased to require of them.
(*Book of Confessions*, 6.012)

This sense of the sovereignty of God has shaped a great deal of Calvinist worship and piety. Presbyterians across the centuries have been uncomfortable with the folksy piety that seems to treat God as a good friend. One of the best expressions of this aspect of Calvinist faith appears in verses one and three in the famous Dutch Reformed hymn, paraphrased by Julia C. Cory, "We Praise Thee, O God, Our Redeemer":

> We praise Thee, O God, our Redeemer, Creator,
> In grateful devotion our tribute we bring.
> We lay it before Thee, we kneel and adore Thee,
> We bless Thy holy name, glad praises we sing.
>
> With voices united our praises we offer,
> And gladly our song of true worship we raise;
> Our sins now confessing, we pray for Thy blessing,
> To Thee, our great Redeemer, ever be praise.

The God of the burning bush is also the one who called Moses, despite his resistance, and the theme of God's calling or election is intimately connected with the Calvinist affirmation of the sovereignty of God. God established a covenant with Moses, just as God had made a covenant with Abraham, and Moses was charged with fulfilling God's purpose. The covenant was initiated by God, and Moses assumed a special calling, sustained by the God who will be with him but will not be completely revealed: "I AM WHO I AM." In this tension of divine intimacy and divine distance lies the paradox of the affirmation of God as sovereign and yet involved with the human condition.

The Calvinist tradition has been littered with the casualties of the debate over election and predestination, but at a basic level the doctrines are meant to affirm central Christian truths. God calls us. God establishes a covenant with us. God saves us, and we do not save ourselves. God promises to be with us. God charges us with special responsibilities for the fulfillment of the divine purpose.

The sovereignty of God has been one of the most potent doctrines in stimulating Calvinist political activism. It lies behind John Knox's famous dictum that he must "obey God rather than any human authority," quoting Peter in Acts 5:29. At the time of the American Revolution, the sovereignty of God formed a central theme of Calvinist preaching in protest against the "oppression"of England. Preachers drew heavily on the Exodus story, likening George Washington to Moses, King George III to pharaoh, and the colonists to the Israelites. The sovereignty of God fueled the protest against slavery and other social injustices. The theme emerged again in the American civil rights movement and in the struggle against apartheid in South Africa.

Fire also becomes a symbol of the Holy Spirit in the account of Pentecost in Acts 2:3–4: "Divided tongues, as of fire, appeared among them, and a tongue rested on each of them. All of them were filled with the Holy Spirit and began to speak in other languages, as the Spirit gave them ability." Pentecost marks the birth of the church through a baptism of fire, and the Holy Spirit gave the apostles the power to proclaim the gospel to people of different lands (2:5–47). Throughout the passage there are the same themes of the revelation by God in the burning bush: the mystery of the flames ("tongues *as of fire*"), God's presence as awe-inspiring, God's blessing on the church, the commissioning of a divine message to be spoken through Peter, and the proclamation of salvation and deliverance.

On Pentecost the Christian church was born, for through the Holy Spirit the salvation of God in Jesus Christ is revealed to us. The Holy Spirit is the soil in which the seed of faith grows and in which the community of faith is nurtured. The church has consistently affirmed that without the work of the Holy Spirit, there can be no faith. But through the Spirit, God's love and forgiveness become real. The Heidelberg Catechism beautifully summarized this affirmation in answering the question of what is faith: "It is not only a certain knowledge by which I accept as true all that God has revealed to us in his Word, but also a wholehearted trust which the Holy Spirit creates in me through the gospel, that, not only to others, but to me also God has given the forgiveness of sins, everlasting righteousness and salvation, out of sheer grace solely for the sake of Christ's saving work" (*Book of Confessions*, 4.021).

The Bible employs the image of fire symbolizing God's presence with a variety of images and with differing emphases. God established a covenant with Abraham in the midst of fire (Gen. 15:17); God remained present with the people of Israel in a pillar of fire that accompanied them by night in the wilderness (Ex. 13:21–22); and God was revealed in the fiery cloud on Mount Sinai where Moses received the law (Ex. 19:16–25; Deut. 4:11–36, 5:4–26).

In the Bible fire also symbolizes God's anger and judgment on the sins of the people. A powerful image is the destruction of Sodom and Gomorrah by fire and brimstone, sent from God (Gen. 19:24–28), but there are many other examples. A dramatic image is the description of God as "a devouring fire, a jealous God" (Deut. 4:24; cf. 9:3). The prophet Isaiah proclaimed, "And the Lord will cause his majestic voice to be heard and the descending blow of his arm to be seen, in furious anger and a flame of devouring fire, with a cloudburst and tempest and hailstones" (30:30). The prophets linked God's judgment in fire to the establishment of justice; for example, Jeremiah proclaimed: "Thus says the Lord: 'Execute justice in the morning, and deliver from the hand of the oppressor anyone who has been robbed, or else my wrath wil' go forth like fire, and burn with no one to quench it, because of your evil doings'" (Jer. 21:12–14; cf. Amos 5:6–7, 7:4).

The fire of God is also related to the biblical imagery of the coming of God to render a final judgment of the world. Isaiah declared, "For the Lord will come in fire, and his chariots like the whirlwind, to pay back his anger in fury, and his rebuke in flames of fire. For by fire will the Lord execute judgment, and by his sword, on all flesh; and those slain by the Lord shall be many" (66:15–16). Jesus used fire to describe a day of judgment in a parable of weeds that will be gathered and cast into a fire (Matt. 13:40–42, 47–50). Paul employed the image to illustrate what will happen when the building materials used by some will prevail and that of others be burned (1 Cor. 3:13–15). And in the book of Revelation, fire is used extensively to convey the power of God's presence and judgment.

At first glance, this violent imagery seems repugnant, and it should be emphasized that these are images. Upon further reflection, however, one recalls that the modern mind has not lost its fascination and preoccupation with fire and destruction. One needs only to examine the "horror" section of a bookstore or videotape rental store or contemplate the power of modern weaponry. It should be remembered also that the imagery of a God of fiery judgment was the vision of God forged by people in persecution, and these passages from the Bible have been used throughout the history of the church to give hope to people who found themselves oppressed by evil and injustice. The God of judgment reaffirmed their belief that the suffering of the innocent and the righteous was not the end of human history.

Fire is frequently associated with sacrifice in the Bible, particularly in the Old Testament where animal sacrifices to God provided a means for purifying people and their relationship to the Lord (cf. Lev. 6:12–13). The connection between sacrifice and suffering was identified with Christian martyrdom, and the image of fire appears frequently in the portrayal of martyrs throughout the history of Christian art.

Fire also purifies and cleanses. In the call of Isaiah to be a prophet, his unclean lips are touched by fiery coals so that he will be able to speak for God (Isa. 6:1–8). Malachi prophesied that a Messiah from God will come and warned: "But who can endure the day of his coming, and who can stand when he appears? For he is like a refiner's fire and like fullers' soap; he will sit as a refiner and purifier of silver, and he will purify the descendants of Levi and refine them like gold and silver, until they present offerings to the Lord in righteousness" (3:2–3).

Fire also may become a symbol for light and truth, which are prevalent images in the New Testament. The prayer Simeon offered after seeing Jesus ("Master, now you are dismissing your servant in peace") concluded with his thanksgiving for "a light for revelation to the Gentiles and for glory to your people Israel" (Luke 2:25–32). Jesus admonished his disciples to be bearers of the good news, for no one would hide a light under a bushel (Luke 8:16–18, 11:33–36). But the image of light has its most extensive use in the Gospel of John and the letters of John. There the Word is the light that has come into the darkness of the world and Jesus is "the light of the world." Those who walk in the light become "children of God" and have "the light of life": "I have come as light into the world that everyone who believes in me should not remain in the darkness" (John 1:1–13, 3:19–21, 8:12–13, 9:4–5, 11:9–10, 12:35–36, 45–46; 1 John 1:5–7).

The image of Jesus as the light of the world has been one of the most powerful metaphors for describing salvation by Christ, and it has its parallels in Paul's description of the sight brought by faith. It has infused the preaching and theology of the church throughout the centuries and had a decisive impact on the language used to describe the missionary expansion of the church. In the image of fire and light lies the same energizing sense of the power of God, who calls us to be witnesses to the love that has claimed us. As the psalmist exclaimed,

> Bless the LORD, O my soul!
> O LORD, my God, you are very great.
> You are clothed with honor and majesty,
>   wrapped in light as with a garment . . .
>
> you make the winds your messengers,
>   fire and flame your ministers.
> (Ps. 104:1–4)

THE TRIANGLE

The implied triangle in the Presbyterian seal is formed by the base of the cross and the bottom and sides of the flames. It is a triangle of equal sides and comes to a peak in the center of the cup, chalice, or baptismal font, as well as the book or Bible.

The triangle has always been used in Christian art to symbolize the Trinity. The task force on the seal specifically asked Malcolm Grear to include a triangle because of the importance of the Trinity in Christian doctrine and the Reformed tradition.

Two ironies stand out immediately whenever people discuss the Trinity. First, the Bible contains no explicit doctrine of the Trinity, even though it has a biblical basis. The idea was gradually developed; the church spoke of it formally at the Council of Nicea in A.D. 325. Second, because of its importance, the Trinity has been the source of extensive and continuing controversy throughout the history of the church. Indeed, one of the major doctrinal differences between Western Christians and many Eastern Orthodox Christians lies in differences concerning the Trinity.

The Trinity is ultimately a mystery, but the concept is crucial in describing the nature of God as one God—"Father, Son, and Holy Spirit" known to us through God's creating, redeeming, and sustaining power over all of life. This mystery of three "persons," or three ways of knowing God, unified in one reality, is at the heart of the idea of the Trinity.

The Christian affirmation of the unity of God comes from the Old Testament and its persistent claim that only Yahweh is Lord. There are no other gods. The people of Israel cannot have any other allegiances. "Hear, O Israel: The LORD is our God, the LORD alone. You shall love the LORD your God with all your heart, and with all your soul, and with all your might" (Deut. 6:4). Old Testament references to God as a Spirit, an angel, the Word of God, and Wisdom also provide suggestions of what Christians have interpreted as the multiple ways of knowing and understanding this one Lord (see, for example, Gen. 1:2; Ex. 23:23; Ps. 33:6; Prov. 8:12ff.; Isa. 48:16).

Although the New Testament does not contain a fully developed doctrine of the Trinity, there is evidence for one. In Matthew's Gospel, Jesus sends out his disciples with this commission: "Go therefore and make disciples of all nations, baptizing them in the name of the Father and of the Son and of the Holy Spirit" (Matt. 28:19). Similarly, when Jesus was baptized, "the Spirit" descended "like a dove on him" and a voice from heaven pronounced, "You are my Son, the Beloved; with you I am well pleased" (Mark 1:10–11). After Jesus read from Isaiah in the synagogue in Nazareth, "The Spirit of the Lord is upon me, because he has anointed me to bring good news to the poor," he announced, "Today this Scripture has been fulfilled in your hearing" (Luke 4:16–21). Jesus offended contemporary sensibilities by using the intimate term "Abba" or "Daddy" for God, and the authors of the Gospels all portray Jesus as explicitly acknowledging his status as God's Son (Matt. 11:27, 16:16–17; Mark 14:61–62; Luke 10:21–22; John 3:34–36, 14:16–17). Jesus further maintained that he will be present with his disciples through the "Advocate" or the Holy Spirit, sent from God (John 14:16–17).

The preaching of Peter and the apostles depended on their understanding of Jesus as the Son of God and the Holy Spirit as God's continuing presence in their lives. For example, when Peter and the apostles were reprimanded for their preaching, they defended themselves with trinitarian language: "The God of our ancestors raised up Jesus, whom you had killed by hanging him on a tree. God exalted him at his right hand as Leader and Savior that he might give repentance to Israel and forgiveness of sins. And we are witnesses to these things, and so is the Holy Spirit whom God has given to those who obey him" (Acts 5:30–32). Similarly, Paul concluded his second letter to the church at Corinth with what is now known as the apostolic benediction: "The grace of the Lord Jesus Christ, and the love of God, and the communion of the Holy Spirit be with all of you" (13:13).

The church has often used the Trinity structure throughout its history in its confessions, most notably in the Apostles' Creed. Calvin organized *The Institutes* in trinitarian fashion, modeling his work on the Apostles' Creed as well. The Presbyterian Church (U.S.A.)'s new confession, "A Brief Statement of Faith," also relies on the trinitarian formula of God.

The new "Brief Statement of Faith" addresses also one major contemporary challenge to the doctrine of the Trinity—the use of masculine language to describe God. In historical debates over the doctrine of the Trinity, the church attempted to preserve the full divinity of each "person" of the Trinity as well as the oneness of God. These debates did not address the problem of referring to God as "Father." Contemporary feminist theologians have questioned the use of this patriarchal term. Many have argued that masculine language about God does not describe adequately a God who transcends human gender, indeed, all finite human definitions of God. On the other hand, many feminist theologians have applauded the doctrine of the Trinity for disclosing God as being plural in nature, as well as one.

The debate over language about God is intense, and it is another example of why Christians have found the doctrine of the Trinity so agonizing and yet so important. "A Brief Statement of Faith" does not ignore the traditional language of the Trinity, but it does make a signal contribution to our understanding of God and the divine drama of redemption. First, it draws on biblical imagery of God as female and male:

> Like a mother who will not forsake her nursing child,
> like a father who runs to welcome the prodigal home,
> God is faithful still. (*Book of Confessions*, 10.3, lines 49–51)

Second, the "Brief Statement" explicitly acknowledges that all people are called by God:

> In sovereign love God created the world good
>> and makes everyone equally in God's image,
>>> male and female, of every race and people,
>> to live as one community.
>> (*Book of Confessions,* 10.3, lines 29–32)

The debate over the Trinity will continue because all our attempts to describe God are human and therefore use finite images to describe an infinite God. The current discussion demonstrates that how we describe God also has implications for how we understand the oneness of the church and the human family. In short, what seems to be another chapter in the history of Christian attempts to describe the mystery of God is also a story with profound ethical implications for Christian discipleship.

The task force on the seal stipulated that the seal should include a triangle also because it could be used to symbolize the idea of the covenant, which has rich biblical roots and has significantly influenced the history of Reformed theology. Basic to the idea of the covenant is God's initiative. God not only created the world but also redeemed it, and through the Holy Spirit, God maintains a continuing relationship with creation. The three points of the triangle can be interpreted in various ways—God/world/humanity, God/church/individual, and so on. The covenant affirms God's involvement with the world and God's refusal to be remote, removed, and unrelated to humanity and the creation. Additionally, the idea of the covenant emphasizes the obligations of humanity to God.

The Old Testament is filled with the language and concept of the covenant. The idea was common to ancient cultures of the Middle East. Although there were covenants or agreements between individuals as equals or between rulers and their subjects, the Old Testament always stressed a special kind of covenant: God's initiative in forming a relationship with the people of Israel. Because they were the people of God, they therefore had certain responsibilities to maintain that relationship and to live in faith.

For example, God established a covenant with Noah, and Noah responded by entering the ark with his family and the animals (Gen. 6:18ff.). After the flood, God made a second covenant with Noah, promising "never again shall there be a flood to destroy the earth" and decreeing that the rainbow shall be the sign or symbol of the covenant (Gen. 9:8–17). In the covenant with Abraham, God promised that Abraham and Sarah would be the parents of many descendants, that this people would be given a land, and that God would remain their God forever. Through them all the nations of the earth would be blessed (Gen. 15–18:15).

In the covenant with Moses, God again issued the pledge to be the God of the people and that they would be delivered from bondage. The covenant included the gift of the law—the structure of God's relationship with the chosen people. The introduction to the Ten Commandments captures this meaning of the covenant as God's bond with the people of Israel: "I am the LORD your God who brought you out of the land of Egypt, out of the house of slavery" (Ex. 20:2). Then followed the commandments themselves.

Writers of the Old Testament understood that the covenant was renewed when David became king and established Israel as a nation. God promised eternal blessing on David and his heirs: "Your house and your kingdom shall be made sure forever before me; your throne shall be established forever" (2 Samuel 7:16). The prophets repeatedly denounced the people of Israel for forsaking the covenant and warned of God's judgment upon them for their faithlessness. But when the people returned to God, as they did in joining Josiah's renewal of the covenant (2 Kings 21–23), then God was merciful and gracious. Ezekiel prophesied "an everlasting covenant" (16:60), and

Jeremiah anticipated "a new covenant" in which God declared: "But this is the covenant that I will make with the house of Israel after those days. . . . I will put my law within them, and I will write it on their hearts; and I will be their God, and they shall be my people" (Jer. 31:31, 33).

Early Christians believed that in the person and in the work of Jesus Christ, God had indeed established the new covenant. Thus, the New Testament writers believed that Jesus was the heir to the covenants with Abraham, Moses, and David, and the fulfillment of the covenants anticipated by the prophets. Jesus' own words instituting the Lord's Supper made such a claim (Luke 22:20; 1 Cor. 11:25). The Lord's Supper became the primary event of Jesus' self-revelation as God's chosen instrument for establishing the new covenant: "While they were eating, Jesus took a loaf of bread, and after blessing it he broke it, gave it to the disciples, and said, 'Take, eat; this is my body.' Then he took a cup, and after giving thanks he gave it to them, saying, 'Drink from it, all of you; for this is my blood of the covenant, which is poured out for many for the forgiveness of sins' " (Matt. 26:26–28; cf. Mark 14:22–25; Luke 22:19b–20; 1 Cor. 11:25).

The early church understood the Lord's Supper as the sacrament in which the community of faith was bound to God and in which they were bound to one another in love. Paul's letters reveal the tensions over whether the law of the old covenant, particularly relating to certain practices and behaviors, was still binding on Christians (for example, Rom. 9–11). Both Paul's letters and the letter to the Hebrews stress that in Christ a new covenant has been established. This covenant has continuity with the covenant with Israel, but it is also a new covenant in being grounded in God's grace in Jesus Christ (for example Gal. 4:21–28; Heb. 7:1–22).

Because of the prominence of covenant as a biblical idea, theologians often used it to describe God's revelation in Jesus Christ. The concept appears often in the writings of Luther and Calvin, but in the late sixteenth and seventeenth centuries, Reformed theologians increasingly used the covenant as the basis for entire theological systems. They contrasted the covenant of works with the covenant of grace; they described the Trinity as a covenant among the three persons of the Trinity. The relationship between believers and God was a covenant—initiated by God and structured by what these Calvinists called God's "eternal decrees." Covenant theology decisively shaped English Puritanism, the Westminster Confession, the Westminster Longer and Shorter Catechisms, and much of American Presbyterianism.

During the seventeenth and eighteenth centuries, when people joined a Calvinist church, they "owned" the covenant—recognizing that they were bound to God and to other believers. Although covenant theologians always insisted that God initiated the covenant, covenant theology raised questions about the role of the will and human initiatives.

Covenant theology emerged in Protestantism at the same time that new forms of contractual thought appeared in Western culture. Covenant theology heavily influenced the idea of representative understandings of church government, and it contributed to the protest against monarchical and hierarchical governments in the English and American revolutions. Many historians have identified covenant theology as one ingredient in the development of constitutions and the modern democratic state.

Covenant theology was unquestionably based on the Bible, but behind it was an impulse to order and structure the life of faith in God's grace. This impulse for order and structure affected the understanding of the church as the covenanted society of believers, the idea of marriage as a compact by two individuals united in love, and the concept of the state and society. Its influence continues into the late twentieth century, but earlier in the century covenant theology had a marked effect on the Presbyterian President Woodrow Wilson and his attempt to reconstruct world politics after the devastation of the First World War.

In interpreting the Covenant of the League of Nations, Wilson declared, "I wish that it were possible for us to do something like some of my very stern ancestors did, for among my ancestors are those very determined persons who were known as the Covenanters. I wish we could, not only for Great Britain and the United States, but for France and Italy and the world, enter into a great league and covenant, declaring ourselves, first of all, friends of mankind and uniting ourselves together for the maintenance and the triumph of right" (John M. Mulder, 274). Wilson's dream was not realized, but his vision continues to inspire those who seek a world governed finally, not by fiat and force, but by common agreement.

Although it may be stretching the limits of symbolism, the triangle also might be interpreted as an image of Presbyterian government. Presbyterians affirm with other Christians the basic doctrines of the Christian faith, but we do have a distinctive understanding of polity. Within Protestantism, Presbyterianism stands between episcopal forms of government with hierarchical structures of power and congregationalism with highly democratic forms of power and authority.

Presbyterian polity is based in large measure on the doctrines of the sovereignty of God and human sinfulness. Because only God is sovereign and because sin pervades every human life, power in the church must be divided. The division of power produces a system of checks and balances. Representatives of the church are given responsibility, but no individual and no one body of the church exercises sole authority for the church, or on behalf of any person. The Presbyterian *Book of Order* quotes the Westminster Confession of Faith in citing its first principle of church order: "God alone is Lord of the conscience" (G–1. 0301).

The three points of the triangle might be seen in various ways: deacon/elder/minister, minister/session/congregation, minister/congregation/presbytery, or presbytery/synod/General Assembly. This division of power can be seen, for example, when a minister is called to a congregation. It is a three-way agreement. The congregation must issue the call, the minister must accept it, and the terms must be approved by the presbytery. Beneath what sometimes seems a rather cumbersome system is an attempt to govern the church through order and balanced authority.

The equilateral triangle does help to suggest an image of the balanced character of the Presbyterian government. The various elements of our polity may not always be equal, but at its best the Presbyterian Church attempts to live a life of faith that is orderly and ordered by God's providence in Jesus Christ.

AFTERWORD

The symbols we have identified in the seal of the Presbyterian Church (U.S.A.) do not exhaust its symbolism or its meaning. There is a sense in which this explication of art violates the principle enunciated by the poet Archibald MacLeish: "A poem should not mean/But be." Others have found and will find new depths and richness in the seal, and that is part of its genius and power as a work of art.

For example, the open cross on the horizontal bars has been seen as a symbol of the church's mission into the world. The cross is not self-contained but open and vulnerable to the world. This open or uncompleted cross can also be a symbol of *"ecclesia reformata, semper reformanda,"* an early Reformed motto for the church reformed but continually being reformed and renewed by God.

The four flames of the Spirit and the three-fold character of the dove add up to seven, the number signifying perfection or perfect order. Seven also may be interpreted as a reference to the seven gifts of the Spirit. In Isaiah 11:2 they are identified as wisdom, understanding, counsel, might, knowledge, and fear of the Lord. Piety was added later. In Revelation 5:12 the seven gifts are power, wealth, wisdom, might, honor, glory, and blessing.

The overall character of the design has reminded some people of the calligraphy of ancient Hebrew and Greek manuscripts. The half circle suggested to another the Pauline description of creation "groaning in labor pains" (Rom. 8:22) for the triumphant return of Christ. Some people have imagined the dove to be a tuft of grain, symbolizing bread and its rich imagery in the Bible as the source of life, as well as the Lord's Supper.

To the dismay of some of my colleagues, I have even jokingly suggested that the dove might be considered a tulip, symbolizing my Dutch heritage and the famous acronym of scholastic Calvinism that came out of the Synod of Dort: TULIP—Total depravity, Unconditional election, Limited atonement, Irresistible grace, and Perseverance of the saints.

When the words "Presbyterian Church (USA)" are used in a circle around the symbol itself, the circle suggests the eternity of God. Designer Malcolm Grear has recommended also that we place the name of the church on three lines beneath the symbol, and the result is an inverted triangle mirroring the triangular character of the symbol itself.

When the cross is rendered in color, it has what Mr. Grear describes as a "throbbing" quality, giving it a vitality that contrasts with the orderliness of the design. The paradox captures the tension in Presbyterianism between *ardor* and *order*. The colors themselves have manifold and rich symbolic meanings. Blue as the color of the sky symbolizes heaven and divine love. Blue can be also a symbol for truth because the blue sky appears when the clouds of doubt are blown away. Red is the color of blood and thus a symbol for Christ, his suffering, and the call to be Christ's disciple. Red is also the color of fire and is associated with Pentecost and God's revelation in the burning bush. Similarly, yellow or gold is the color of the sun and symbolizes God and the majesty of God. White symbolizes innocence, purity, and holiness. It is frequently associated with biblical references to Christ at the transfiguration wearing a robe of "dazzling white" (Matt. 17:2) or after his resurrection wearing "clothing white as snow" (Matt. 28:3). But it is also associated with the power of God's love to cleanse people from sin: "Wash me, and I shall be whiter than snow" (Ps. 51:7).

But to me, the most interesting aspect of the seal of the Presbyterian Church is the three-fold character of the cross itself, and in that design is a piece of the history of the Presbyterian

Church that Mr. Grear and his associates did not know. It is also a chapter that has a unique relationship to my family and explains why this symbol means so much to me.

The formation of the Presbyterian Church (U.S.A.) was actually the union of three churches in the mid to late twentieth century. The Presbyterian Church in the United States of America (PCUSA) and the United Presbyterian Church of North America (UPCNA) merged in 1958 to form the United Presbyterian Church in the United States of America. That United Presbyterian Church and the Presbyterian Church in the U.S. (PCUS) merged in 1983 to form our present denomination.

The century-long division in American Presbyterianism was spawned by the Civil War, and one of the great Northern leaders of the effort to heal the breach was my childhood pastor, Dr. Harrison Ray Anderson, for many years the pastor of the Fourth Presbyterian Church in Chicago. Early in his ministry, Dr. Anderson was reading the history of the Presbyterian Church, and he discovered that his great grandfather was the man who had championed the so-called Spring Resolutions at the 1861 General Assembly. These resolutions essentially called for Southern Presbyterians to pledge their allegiance to the Union. They became the precipitating cause of the withdrawal of Southern presbyteries and the formation of the Presbyterian Church in the Confederate States of America, later the Presbyterian Church in the U.S.

Anderson repeatedly told the story of reading a history of the Presbyterian Church, and how, when he realized his great-grandfather had been the key figure in the passage of the Spring Resolutions, he fell on his knees and asked God to make him an instrument in bringing the two churches together. He labored from the 1930s until his death in 1979 for the cause of Presbyterian union, and he was one of the few Northern Presbyterians who received a hearing in the South. Although he died before he saw his dream realized, he left a symbolic legacy, which the seal of the Presbyterian Church embodies.

The beginning of that legacy lies in the early months of World War II. After the attack on Pearl Harbor, there was a near-hysterical fear of Japanese who were living in the United States. This fear ultimately produced the tragedy of the incarceration of many Japanese-American citizens in concentration camps, one of the most flagrant violations of civil rights in this nation's history.

In Chicago at the beginning of the war, a small group of Japanese-American Christians were forced out of the church in Hyde Park where they were worshiping. They came to the Fourth Presbyterian Church and asked Anderson for permission to worship there. Fourth was one of the most important Protestant churches in Chicago, with many prominent civic leaders in its membership, and it was the largest Presbyterian church in the city. Anderson referred the request to a committee of the session, composed of my father, John Mulder, my godfather, Dr. Stewart Thomson, and another man.

At the next meeting of the session, the committee unanimously recommended that the Japanese-American congregation be allowed to worship in the church. A violent and emotional debate erupted; the horrible passions stirred by the war arose in the arguments. At one point my godfather threatened to resign from the session and leave the church if the session failed to sustain the committee's recommendation. The session adjourned without reaching any decision and convened again a week later. Finally, Dr. Anderson took the vote, and the recommendation was approved by a majority of one.

On Sunday afternoons throughout the war, Dr. Anderson, dressed in a clerical gown, often stood at the side entrance to the church where the Japanese-Americans entered and exited from the worship service in the chapel. He did so, he said, to prevent them from any harassment by passersby.

At the end of the war, the Japanese-American congregation presented Dr. Anderson with a gift of money in gratitude for what he and Fourth Church had done for them. Shortly thereafter, Dr. Anderson left for a trip to Scotland and the island of Iona, where he purchased two small, silver Celtic crosses with the money he had been given by the Japanese. When he returned to the United States, he presented one cross to the moderator of the PCUSA and another to the moderator of the PCUS. Later he presented a third cross to the moderator of the UPCNA. In making the presentations, he expressed the hope that someday these three crosses would be welded together as one. These crosses became the symbol of the office of moderator, and each moderator wore one.

In 1958, when the UPCNA and the PCUSA merged, two of the crosses were bound together. And in a dramatic moment in Atlanta in 1983, an Asian jeweler—with hands trembling—welded the three crosses together on the platform of the General Assembly in front of more than five thousand Presbyterians.

The symbol of the moderator is now three crosses that have become one. The seal of our church is a three-fold cross, and behind this symbolism is the story of a church that befriended an oppressed group of people in their time of need. From that group came the crosses that are now bound together, embodying Calvin's hope that the unity of the church "ought to be such that we form one body and one soul." In that common witness lies also the mission of a church to reach out to precisely those people whose needs are great but who could so easily be shunned.

In the story behind the seal is a symbol and a summons to what the church could be.

77

WORKS CITED

Brown, Robert McAfee. *The Spirit of Protestantism.* New York: Oxford University Press, 1961.

Calvin, John. *Institutes of the Christian Religion,* ed. John T. McNeill, trans. Ford Lewis Battles, 2 vols. Louisville, Ky.: Westminster/John Knox Press, 1960.

The Constitution of the Presbyterian Church (U.S.A.), Part I: *Book of Confessions.* Louisville, Ky.: Office of the General Assembly, 1991.

The Constitution of the Presbyterian Church (U.S.A.), Part II: *Book of Order.* Louisville, Ky.: Office of the General Assembly, 1990.

Mulder, John M. *Woodrow Wilson.* Princeton, N.J.: Princeton University Press, 1978.

Our Confessional Heritage: Confessions of the Reformed Tradition with a Contemporary Declaration of Faith, Presbyterian Church in the United States. Atlanta, Ga.: Office of the General Assembly, 1978.